Profit Equalizer

Exclusive Step-By-Step Guide Reveals...

"How To Utterly Devastate Your Competition, While Growing Your Business By Leaps and Bounds Starting Almost Overnight!"

By Jeff Alderson

From Business Transforming Marketing Strategies to Pay-Per-Click Search Engines, Even The Basics of Search Engine Optimization... You Will Learn The Ins and Outs Of Step-By-Step Wiping Out Your Competition!

With These New Strategies In Your Hands, You'll Gain The Power To Effortlessly Take Your Business To The Next Level... Growing From Your Current Results To a Fair Monopoly. Your Profits Can Easily Double By Simply Using Any of The Countless Strategies Inside!

Legal Disclaimer

The creators of Profit Equalizer and Xybercode, Inc. have created this ebook and the program using their best efforts. Said creators, authors and publishers make no representations or warranties, neither expressed nor implied, as to the accuracy, applicability, fitness or completeness of the program's contents.

There are no warranties, either expressed or implied, as to the merchantability or fitness of this program for any particular purpose and they shall in no event be held liable for any damages or other loss, including, but not limited to, special, incidental, consequential, and/or other damages. Whenever you are starting a business venture, including affiliate marketing, you should consult with legal, tax, and accounting professionals.

The creators of Profit Equalizer and Xybercode, Inc. do not warrant the performance, applicability, or effectiveness of any of the companies or websites mentioned in this ebook. All links and references are for informational purposes only and are not warranted in any way, for any reason.

The material contained within this ebook is protected under International and Federal Copyright Laws and Treaties, and as such, any unauthorized reprint or use of this material is strictly prohibited.

The names of other products and services referred to in Profit Equalizer may be trademarks or copyrights of their respective owners. There is no affiliation, endorsement, or sponsorship by owners of trademarked or copyrighted products or services.

Dear Friend,

We've all done it…

Gotten excited about some money-making program or system that came our way. After all, it's hard not to when there are so many of them out there. No matter how reserved or hesitant you are - no matter how skeptical you might be - sooner or later something will strike a cord deep down in your soul.

Maybe it was pointed out to you by a friend or business associate you trusted. Or maybe it was recommended by some internet marketing expert or guru you greatly admired. Either way, the money-making strategy they've put you on to really does sound like the next best super-duper income-producing method… one you couldn't possibly turn away from.

You try to ignore the hype, the sales pitch. But there's something that catches your eye, something that makes you pause just long enough to think, *is it really possible…* Whatever it is, you decide to take a closer look.

So you click on the link, read the sales copy, get impressed by all the glowing testimonials that verify this is in fact a can't-lose, make-money-while-you-sleep kind of deal, one that any intelligent individual would be insane NOT to take advantage of.

Do you remember how it felt? That rush, that high… that feeling that you were only a stone's throw away from generating the kind of income you had only previously dreamed about? Yep… you could feel it in your bones. This was definitely IT. The opportunity you had been searching, hoping, waiting for.

You were pumped, you were psyched… you were literally chomping at the bit to run this particular race to the finish line!

And since you couldn't wait to get started, you immediately hit the order button. Within minutes, you had the information in hand… the process that would finally - once and for all - lead you directly to your ultimate goal…

FINANCIAL FREEDOM!

Now let's fast forward to a few days (or maybe a few weeks) later.

You've finished absorbing all the instructions, all the advice, all the steps that will place you in a position to earn unlimited income. You've even managed to implement some of the first stages of this money-making system. But in the process, some of the "shine" has begun to fade. Although you're still optimistic, you're not QUITE as psyched as you were in the very beginning, when the whole money-making scenario was merely a mental image.

You… lounging on the beach of a tropical island. You… sitting behind the wheel of a $200,000 sports car. You… dressed in designer clothes and attending posh exclusive parties of the rich and famous.

That's the kind of pot-of-gold, end-of-the-rainbow lifestyle the guy who wrote the sales copy told you to imagine. And you did, right up until the time you actually started to invest real time and effort, started to "work" toward that vision.

Nonetheless, you still want desperately to see this through to the finish, to prove you've got the metal, the right stuff. After all, there's that pot of gold waiting at the end of this rainbow. And that's when it hits you. Pot of gold? Isn't that where the devious (albeit imaginary) leprechaun hid his own fortune?

Whatever commitment you originally had is now replaced with stark reality. There is no pot of gold, no magical mystical means of getting rich. You either inherit a fortune, win the lottery, or rob a bank. That's it.

Oh sure. Some people strike it rich online (or, at the very least, become financially comfortable). But that's just a fluke, something that only happens to a fraction of a percentage of all the people who pursue the dream of becoming financially independent via the internet. Right?

Well, yes and no.

While it's true that only a small percentage of people succeed online, it's also very true that the opportunity to succeed is available to EVERYONE who makes the attempt. Let me repeat that last statement…

The opportunity to succeed is available to EVERYONE who makes the attempt.

Of course, there's a very important kicker attached to that statement. You have to know exactly what money-making systems will actually succeed. And yes, regardless of what some might have you believe, there ARE in fact several ways in which the average person can become financially successful online.

Are any of them attached to some sort of "free ride"? You know, where you put some genius system in place and money just automatically starts jamming your bank account?

Sorry to burst your bubble - to finally dispel what so many have promised you time and time again - but there is no method that even comes close. Instead, each and every solid money making system requires that a certain degree of time and effort be invested. Some more than others, but required investment nevertheless.

Now, before you get all frustrated and disappointed, be assured that the method you're about to learn is one that requires the least amount of time and effort. AND, once the system is in place, it basically runs itself. Not entirely, of course. But enough that only a few hours (or less) will be required for weekly maintenance.

In other words, you do a small amount of work to get things set up, to get the system rolling, and then simply put in the minimal amount of time it takes to keep the whole operation running smoothly and productively.

Of course, once you experience that first burst of income, there's no way you'll want to simply "coast" along. Most likely, you'll dig in your heels and keep duplicating that same system, over and over again, developing multiple streams of income.

And the good news is, once you become comfortable with the process, each new money-making system is a piece of cake. Merely a process of repeating what you've previously done. And naturally, the more times you repeat the process, the more money you'll make.

So what exactly IS this solid money-making system?

You're probably on the edge of your seat, expecting some sort of complicated, secretive James Bond answer that only a handful of savvy internet marketing experts know about. If that's what you think, you're half right.

The truth is, savvy (and wealthy) internet marketing experts not only know about this, they've been doing it for years. That's right. While everyone else is out there chasing their own tail, jumping on each and every get-rich scheme that comes down the internet pike, a select group of marketers have been slowly - almost doggedly - developing one money-making system after the other.

Year after year, they continue to bring in substantial income. And unlike other methods, theirs will never fall apart or become obsolete or be replaced by some "better" system. Why? Because their method IS the better system. Always was, always will be.

Granted, there are new twists being added all the time - no different than keeping up with the latest trends, technology, and customer demands. But the system itself? That's rock solid… regardless of what the search engines do or don't do, regardless of how many new or "popular" money-making ideas come and go. This system has the ultimate staying power.

On top of that, the system you're about to learn isn't complicated. Nor is it secretive. At least, the overall concept isn't some deep dark secret known only to a few chosen marketers. What IS important are the components that make up the system.

Do it right and you'll be generating income for as long as you want. Get it wrong - take a few shortcuts or leave out key ingredients - and you can toss any chance of financial freedom right out the window.

But let's not even consider any such negative concepts. You wouldn't even be here if you weren't serious. So let's get serious, shall we? Let's get right down to the nuts and bolts of the <u>only</u> money-making system you'll ever need!

Profit Equalizer Overview

The true power of the internet lies in one's ability to connect with millions of people all over the world. That means there is no limit to the number of eyes that will see your product, your business, your offer.

Basically, the internet provides a playing field that is equal to all participants. Anyone who comes online has the same advantage, the same possibilities, the same avenues.

What's not equal is how people operate online. Some choose physical products, others choose services, and still others get into money-making systems like multi-level marketing (MLM) and affiliate programs. And although any one of them can generate a good deal of income, they offer the average person very little chance of being financially successful.

Of course, the majority of people who come online in hopes of generating great wealth from the comfort of their home don't have a clue what's really involved. And the fact that the internet is a vast breeding ground for misinformation doesn't help either.

Everywhere you turn, someone is hawking a get-rich-quick scheme. Or some method of taking shortcuts to the online treasure chest (in this case, the treasure chest is financial success). The truth is, there are no shortcuts. And the only person who can get rich quick is the person selling the get-rich-quick scheme.

The only part you can honestly count on is the treasure chest. Why? Because it really does exist. And there are only two things you need in order to get hold of it: 1) the keys that unlock each of the doors which lead to the treasure chest, and 2) the system that allows you to use those keys quickly and effectively.

That's what Profit Equalizer is all about. Handing you the keys that will open each of the doors standing between you and financial success. We'll get into all the specifics in a few minutes, but first, let's run through a brief overview of the Profit Equalizer system.

For the most part, there are three primary components: preparation, purpose, and profit.

- Preparation - you get everything set up.
- Purpose - you concentrate on a specific product.
- Profit - you generate traffic and implement promotion techniques.

If you think this sounds familiar, you're right. It's the basis for every profitable business venture. The only difference is, Profit Equalizer focuses on generating income through a very precise and specific sequence of events... point A leads to point B which leads to point C, and so on and so on.

It's not complicated by any means. It's merely a system that has proven time and time again to bring in substantial amounts of money. Assuming, of course, that you actually follow and then implement the system.

That being said, here's an overview of Profit Equalizer. It involves...

- Fundamental basis
- Central core
- Variable flexibility
- Ultimate wealth and success

The *fundamental basis* of the system is the fact that you will have total control over the amount of income you generate. The system shows you HOW to generate the income, but you determine how much and how often.

The actual *central core* of the system is a targeted, high-demand digital information product. Surrounding the product is a totally automated process that presents, promotes, sells, and delivers it to equally targeted and hungry consumers.

The *variable flexibility* of the system means you can operate it from a one-person perspective, whereby you take care of all the tasks yourself. Or, you can operate through a management position, whereby you outsource repetitive and time-consuming things like set-up, performance, and promotion tasks to hired individuals.

The *ultimate wealth and success* of the system lies in the fact that the process can easily be duplicated over and over again, each time with a different yet still highly targeted in-demand digital information product.

Overall, the Profit Equalizer system is simple and direct, a method that anyone can use to gain online financial success. Most importantly, it is extremely effective in generating income week after week, month after month, year after year.

Keep in mind, however, that it's only the overall concept of Profit Equalizer that is simple. The method by which it's utilized (the individual and sequence of keys that are involved) is the true guaranteed money maker.

The only possible limitation is the one you yourself might impose...

Without a doubt, the most difficult part of this system is getting started. Not because it's a difficult system to implement but rather because most people can't seem to get that initial momentum going. What they generally do is look to the end of the rainbow (after all, that's what all the experts tell you to do - envision the lifestyle you'll soon be living).

Unfortunately, that type of thinking has a tendency to paralyze most people. They're so engrained in imagining their life draped in wealth, they begin to see the path that will get them there as this long, unending road. Without even having started the journey, they begin adding up all the steps involved, all the tasks they need to accomplish.

What started out as a possible dream winds up becoming this incredibly overwhelming pile of work that needs to be done. *What was I thinking? How can I possibly do all this?* No doubt, it's a terrible feeling, especially when you consider how pumped and psyched you were in the beginning.

So how do you prevent that "letdown" from happening? Simple...

1. Don't think about the end of the road. That wealthy lifestyle you're hoping to achieve can motivate or cripple you, depending on how much emphasis you place on it. Yes, it's nice to have a dream, but there's a time to dream and a time to dig in your heels and get things done. Now that you have the Profit Equalizer system in hand, it's time to dig in your heels and get things done.

2. Don't think about the entire system as a whole. Instead, concentrate on one step at a time. Once you've accomplished the first step, move on to the next one. That way, the process won't seem quite as daunting or overwhelming. It's not. It's simply a matter of doing one thing and then another - one step in front of the other - until you reach your destination.

The bottom line... don't get ahead of yourself. The reason so many online marketers continue to generate steady streams of income is simply because they took it one step at a time. And once they had their initial money-making system in place, they took a quick breath and began building the next one.

Here's another thing... it's not necessarily a good thing to be in a big rush. Granted, the sooner you get things in place, the sooner you'll make money. What you don't want to do, though, is put too much pressure on yourself. If you just believe that you'll get there - and keep pressing forward - you WILL get there.

Set a pace that's comfortable for you personally (if possible, set up an actual schedule that commits you to "x" amount of hours "x" amount of days every week - and then stick to it as best you can). Take your time, take things one step at a time. That way, you'll not only be able to move steadily forward, you won't be paralyzed into not moving at all.

Understood? Great. Now let's get to the individual keys - and remember - ONE step at a time...

Key No. 1: Establish Your Financial Goal

You've heard it all before. In order to walk among the rich and famous, you need to first define your personal goals. You know, make a list of everything you want in life, everything you want to accomplish.

Well, you'll be happy to know, that's NOT the kind of thing we're talking about here.

There are plenty of books out there that will teach you how to be a winner, how to think like the rich, how to develop the proper mind-set. No one's saying those types of things aren't important with regard to achieving financial success. They are. They just don't happen to be the subject of this particular key.

What we're talking about here is a dollar figure, a specific amount that you set as your daily income goal. Basically, you need to determine how much money you would need to generate each day in order to quit your job, in order to earn money exclusively from home.

Before you come up with any sort of dollar figure, though, a word of caution. The figure needs to be high enough that you can live comfortably, but it also needs to be low enough that it's entirely realistic. You know, doable.

For example, you might ultimately want to make over a thousand dollars a day. And there's certainly nothing wrong with that. You just don't want to set the bar so high at the very beginning that you feel overly pressured.

So what you need to do is be totally honest with yourself. Set a financial goal that will be high enough to give you proper incentive and keep you motivated but isn't so high that it prevents you from accomplishing your goal amount.

For some people, the "magic" figure might be as low as $50 a day, which in turn equates to $1500 a month. Others might wish to set a minimum that's considerably higher. (With this particular system, most everyone can aspire to at least $100 a day.)

The point is, only you know what you need. And more importantly, what you're capable of accomplishing. Plus, anyone who is currently holding down an outside job and can only invest a few hours throughout the week to start with should probably set a relatively reasonable daily financial goal.

Adversely, someone who has the ability to work fulltime at getting this system set up and running can probably establish a much higher daily dollar amount.

Regardless, it's important that you do in fact choose a specific financial goal. Then, once you've achieved that amount, you can raise the stakes. So the process is... you reach a dollar figure, set another financial goal, reach that dollar figure, set another financial goal, and so on.

Whatever you do, though, don't put a time limit on WHEN you have to achieve your financial goals. The dollar amount itself is the target, NOT how long it takes you to get there. This is extremely important. So don't dismiss it as irrelevant or minimal.

You see, the reason most people fail (aside from the fact that they either don't know how to succeed or never find a good solid money-making product, system, or program) is simply because they place too much pressure on themselves. The bar is set so high, they can't possibly reach it, let alone scale it.

It's great to have dreams. It's wonderful to envision a lifestyle that has no financial worries or concerns. But if you wind up putting an insurmountable wall between you and the lifestyle you've always wanted, the dream will never be realized.

Of course, that's not going to happen here. You're going to set a financial amount and then concentrate on achieving that dollar figure. That's the goal.

That's also Key No. 1 in the money-making system. Key No. 2 discusses the easiest means of generating your income.

Key No. 2: The Easiest Income Generator

There's a reason the World Wide Web is referred to as the information highway. It just happens to be a place where you can find out just about anything there is to know...

Would you like to learn how to knit or crochet? How to grow the perfect rose? Do you need directions to a specific establishment in a certain town? Are you looking for dating or romance tips? What about instructions on how to build a dog house or teaching your parrot to talk or do tricks?

If your brain can come up with it, the information can most likely be found somewhere on the internet. But the important aspect of this is the fact that at any given moment, in a place somewhere around the globe, someone is searching for information about something.

And that's exactly why fortunes are being made by those who are selling information products. In fact, for the majority of financially successful online marketers, it's the number one choice.

Why would anyone pay for information, something that is already available for free? That depends. In some instances, it's merely the benefit of all aspects of a certain topic or subject matter being offered in one easy location (as opposed to someone having to search high and low). Or, some area of information might be included that isn't freely or readily available elsewhere.

And of course, there are publications like this one which reveal a specific method of making money. It doesn't really matter. As long as there are people searching for information, products that provide valuable and interesting content will always generate revenue.

The most critical aspect, however, is on the side of the seller. Information can be delivered digitally. Things like inventory, packaging and shipping, and physical delivery are non-existent. And because of all that, digital information products allow for the highest possible profit margin.

Saving time is another important factor. More specifically, saving

YOUR time. With a digital product, the sales, purchase, and delivery process can all be totally automated. You set it up once and it continues to bring in revenue for as long as you leave it in place. And that leaves you free to spend time and effort where it's most needed... promotion and marketing.

When it comes to deciding what type of digital product (the subject matter), the field is wide open. No matter what topic of information you think of, someone somewhere is searching for it. That's not to say all information is valuable. It's not.

Your priority is to deal in topics that are not only in demand by consumers but are also capable of generating cash. In other words, a large number of consumers are willing to pay to get that information.

But before we get to that point (that's Key No. 3), you need to look around the internet and see what other information products people are currently selling. There's no limit to what's out there so you'll easily be exposed to each and every possible area of interest.

When it comes to making money through information products, almost every conceivable topic and area of interest needs to be considered. After all, thanks to the internet, you have the capability of reaching every possible audience...

There are people involved with sports, finance, construction, pets, gambling, housing, romance, health, diets, science, aliens, gardening, parenting, counseling... you name it, there's a group of individuals who have an interest in it.

And as long as there's enough people interested in a particular activity, topic, or subject matter, money can be made by providing associated information. But please, whatever you do, don't even consider limiting yourself to the field of internet marketing or the business of making money at home.

Yes, these are highly sough-after and profitable online areas. But there's also the MOST competition going on within these fields. So unless you can come up with some really killer, blockbuster, never-been-heard-of-before information, you might want to leave this area alone. At least until you get more comfortable and experienced with the entire system.

Instead, look to areas that are more common to the average person. Things like cooking, dog training, craft projects, weight loss, health products. Not because you might be getting into those types of areas but because you need to become comfortable with digital information products in general.

True, you might think you're already familiar with them. But it's important that you spend some extra time cruising the internet with digital products as your sole objective. Keep in mind… information products will be at the very core of your money-making system. Like any business, the more you know about your product, the farther ahead you'll be in developing your own successful income producing system.

Once you feel you're totally and completely familiar with all aspects of digital information products, it's time to start drilling down into specific target areas. Which brings us to Key No. 3.

Key No. 3: Check The Pulse Of Consumers

Look at a news or magazine stand. Take a walk down a city street or through the park. Watch television commercials. Watch infomercials. Talk to your friends, your family members, your business associates, your co-workers.

Anywhere you go, anyone you talk to can lead to the information you're looking for. And that is... exactly what people are hungry for. But most importantly, what they're hungry for right now.

It's doesn't really matter what the rage was ten years ago, or even ten months ago. Is it popular NOW? Are people currently doing this, that, or the other thing? If it turns out they're only doing the other thing, then forget about this or that.

Always pay attention to what's going on around you, what you see, what you read, what people are talking about...

What's the latest trend, the latest fashion, the latest interest? What kind of articles, questions, and information keeps cropping up time and time again? What particular topics or areas of interest seem to jump out at you or make you take a second look?

Go to discussion boards (forums) and chat rooms and be a fly on the wall. Take note of what people are complaining about, the problems they're having, the kind of information or products they wish was available to them.

Start documenting specific topics or subject areas that keep cropping up. If you think a particular product or area of information looks promising, add it to the list of possibilities. It doesn't matter what it's related to - pet care, health industry, magic tricks, home-grown vegetables, breast reduction, hair restoration - if you've discovered that the topic currently holds interest for a large group of people, it warrants a closer look.

Your ultimate goal will be to establish anywhere from three to five specific income-producing areas of interest. For right now, though, it's important to gather as many possibilities as you can. Once you begin to dig deeper and conduct specific research (Key No. 4), many of the items on your list will wind up being eliminated. So the more you have to work with, the better your chance of whittling the list down to that minimum three to five topics of interest (those are the money-makers you'll work with first).

Although you might be tempted to, please don't take this part of the system lightly. Every financially successful person makes a point of being on top of the latest trends and ideas. If something happens in their industry or area of expertise, they're immediately aware of it. And because of that, they're always capable of releasing the next hot product.

Follow in their footsteps and you'll always have a new digital information product to add to your profit-generating system. Of course, before you can release any new product, you need to conduct the proper research.

Your primary objective in that respect is to determine whether or not the product - and the area of interest it's associated with - will equate to earning a substantial amount of income. And what's important to realize here is that the most popular topic and the hottest product might not necessarily produce the largest amount of income.

Of course, that's the whole purpose of conducting research… to find out what topics - and therefore what digital information products - would be your best financial choices.

And that's what we're going to talk about next.

Key No. 4: Conduct Proper Research

Now that you've compiled a list of specific topics of interest to work with, it's time to find out which ones are most likely to generate cash income. And to do that, a certain amount of research will be necessary.

The priority here is to determine what people are searching for on a monthly basis as well as how many times that particular topic and areas of interest within that topic are being searched for. The more searches that are being conducted, the more potential there is for generating income.

Of course, sheer numbers are only one aspect of that final determination. You also have to consider how much competition you're facing. For example, let's say your chosen topic is dogs. Within that topic - and after having conducted the proper amount of research - you've initially determined that the subject of "dog training" appears to be a very strong possibility for generating income.

If, on further investigation, you discover that there is way too much competition already out there - that too many people are already selling dog training manuals and information - you might need to reconsider that particular choice.

On the other hand, you might have located a digital product that sells information which is highly specific to a unique or unusual dog training device or system. If it turned out there was little or no competition for that type of information, it would then automatically qualify as a solid income generator.

Basically, it's a matter of looking at each topic of interest from several different angles... the number of people who search for it every month, relevant information products that are available, and the level of competition that's already out there.

One of the best research utilities is Ad Word Analyzer. This program will quickly and easily help you take a deeper look at what people are searching for. And it does it by automatically digging up the search terms and then providing research data for each of them.

As you get further into the Profit Equalizer system, you'll find that Adword Analyzer is one of the most valuable and efficient tools you can use. For initial research, however, you merely need to determine how many people are searching for individual and specific search terms (keywords) each month.

For that type of research, there's a free online keyword suggestion tool that's located at the following URL address:

http://inventory.overture.com/d/searchinventory/suggestion

Since you'll be using this tool quite frequently, you might want to add it to your favorites or create a shortcut on your computer desktop.

From your list of topics, type one into the form field that's entitled "Get suggestions for". The results that come back are twofold. First, you'll see a list of all the search terms that include the word you typed in. Second, you can click on any one of those individual terms and another list will come up, one that includes all the variations of that particular term.

For example, if your topic was "health" and you typed that word into the Overture form field, the first results you received would include terms like "health insurance", "health care", "mental health", and "health fitness".

If you click on "health fitness", terms such as "health and fitness articles", "health and fitness magazine", "health fitness club", and "health fitness gyms" will be displayed in the next page of search results.

Now you know what terms are being search for within the health topic. What's most important about conducting this type of search, however, is the fact that next to every search term is a number. And that number tells you how many people searched for that particular term over the course of an entire month.

Armed with that type of information, you can then easily determine whether or not your topic is even worth pursuing. Once you determine that, you have to look at the keyword results and see whether or not there's a particular area of interest within that topic that would qualify as something which would generate a substantial amount of income.

Here are the three basic qualifiers for a specific area of interest:

1. A large number of people conduct searches for it every month.
2. Current competition is relatively low (or at least in the moderate range).
3. An information product that's associated with the topic is available.

If your topic - as well as a specific area of interest within that topic - meets all three of these criteria, you've got a prime candidate for generating substantial income.

Continue to go through all the topics on your list, organizing them in terms of which ones have the most potential with regard to making money and those which seem to have the least amount of potential. (From this new list, you'll be working your way down from the top.)

Now that you know what topics and areas of interest are most suitable for generating income, you'll need to see what information products are available for each of those topics. We'll do that next.

Key No. 5: Acquiring Information Products

As previously mentioned, digital information products are the central core of the Profit Equalizer system. Acquiring ones that will generate solid income streams is therefore extremely important.

Naturally, you've already determined the areas of interest that will generate income. So the next thing you're going to do is locate quality products that people who are searching in those areas of interest would be anxious to purchase.

Notice the word "anxious".

That means they're not just willing to buy the product, they are highly motivated to do so. Granted, not every product will bring in an extraordinary amount of money. Some will, some won't. But that's not the point.

You want to look at - and ultimately choose - products that automatically push certain consumer buttons, that naturally prompt potential buyers into making the purchase. And when you think about it, that won't be too difficult a task. After all…

You've already determined which areas of interest are most sought after. Information that is directly related to those areas is therefore pre-qualified. But that's not the only thing you need to consider when choosing the "right" information products.

We'll get into the specific choices you have for acquiring information products in a few minutes, but for right now, let's assume you've decided to sell someone else's information product as the core of one of your money-making systems.

Since you basically want something that sells itself (as opposed to having to convince potential buyers), you need to look at the sales copy and overall presentation that goes along with it. Would YOU buy the product? If not - if the sales content is under-whelming or in some way inferior - you'll have two choices…

1. Forget about that particular product.
2. Create your own more compelling sales content.

Mind you, with <u>any</u> information product you sell, it's important to establish your own sales pitch and/or presentation. That way, you have total control over what keywords are targeted throughout the content (extremely important with regard to search engine optimization).

In other words, even if you're merely selling a product as an affiliate, and even if the owner of that product has written a killer sales page, you still need to develop your own presentation - on your own web page or pages. We'll get into all that further on as well, but for right now, let's concentrate on the product itself.

In general, there are four primary methods in which to acquire information products.

1. Become a sales affiliate for an existing product.
2. Develop a private joint venture with the owner of a product.
3. Create your own product.
4. Pay someone to create products for you.

For the first choice, ClickBank is one of the best places to find digital information products. They're even organized by categories such as education, publishing, health, fitness, diet, cooking, recipes, sports, recreation, music, etc. Plenty of digital products to choose from. In fact, you can actually go to ClickBank's marketplace and get some great ideas for topics and areas of interest.

Plus, the products in each category are listed according to popularity (letting you know which products are being promoted the most by other affiliates). Having that type of information will help you select products that are in a less competitive arena.

And since ClickBank has their own affiliate program, you can sell whatever product you like simply by using their custom affiliate link (which includes both your ClickBank user ID and that of the product being sold).

For more information about this and all their other features, check out their website at http://www.clickbank.com.

The second choice - developing a private joint venture - is a bit more complicated and requires much more time and effort. However... it's one of the most powerful methods of generating the largest amount of revenue. That's assuming, of course, you take the time necessary to choose wisely.

If you're not already aware, there are plenty of junk information products floating around out there. Before you even consider establishing a partnership with someone (a product joint venture), you need to be certain that both they and their product are reputable.

Once you've located a good product, one that you feel would be a suitable fit for your particular area of interest, you need to purchase that product. Why? Because there's no way to be certain how good or bad it is without actually reading it.

Then, if it meets your approval, you'll need to send the owner a joint venture proposal. There are various free proposal letter samples available online so you're sure to find a good one that will work as a template for your own correspondence.

At the very least, a joint venture proposal letter should include the following characteristics:

- Highly personalized to the individual you're writing to.
- Giving praise to their product (you DID buy and read it didn't you?).
- Why/how this joint venture would benefit both of you (but mostly them).
- Offering them a percentage deal that's above and beyond the average.
- The type of advertising/promotion their product will receive in your hands.
- Your credentials/expertise in selling information products (if any).
- The means by which you can discuss it further (at THEIR

convenience).

Since you'll most likely be sending the proposal via email, you'll need a good subject line. Whatever you do... never, NEVER, use something shocking, cutesy, or hyped up.

Instead, your subject line should state your exact intention (assuming the prospect's first name is John)... "John - A Joint Venture Proposal" or John - JV Proposal for your consideration".

That's it. Nothing more, nothing less. Why? Because the type of person you're writing to is busy. They don't have time to go through every email they receive. If you hype up the subject line, it could very well be trashed as junk mail. This way, the recipient knows exactly what to expect and will view it as valid and professional correspondence.

Your next choice for acquiring information products is to create your own. If you have the time and the ability to do so, it's a good choice. Otherwise, you could be wasting effort that should be invested in other areas of the system.

Time is money. Use it wisely. And that brings us to the final choice...

Hire someone else to create information products for you. While this might seem like a rather costly avenue to take, it has the potential of earning you much more revenue over the course of the ensuing months or even years.

Where most people go wrong in this area is choosing the wrong topic. If you're considering the possibility of hiring someone else, make absolutely certain you've done your homework, your research. If you do, the information product will serve you well over a long period of time, far exceeding the cost of having it written for you.

Another benefit is the fact that owning your own products means you'll have total control over them. You don't need to share profits and you don't need to ask someone if you decide to offer things like trial versions, discount pricing, and so forth.

You might be wondering why the subject of reprint (or resale) rights wasn't included in this particular section. That's because most products where reprint rights are available have already be promoted to death. First by the owner and then by everyone who has gotten hold of the rights to resell the product.

Of course, if you can strike up some sort of "exclusive" resale option for a product you've located by all means do so. But then, that would basically put the deal into the joint venture category rather than the purchase of resell rights.

Regardless, you should always be somewhat wary of any product "rights" that are being sold publicly. In most instances, they're being offered simply because the majority of income has already been earned from the sale of that particular product. Reprint rights are - for the most part - the owner's final attempt at generating another last-ditch cash flow.

Ok. That pretty much sums up the topic of acquiring information products. Now let's talk about how you should market each of the products you've chosen.

Key No. 6: Get The Right Vantage Point

As previously mentioned, you can become an affiliate and sell products that other people own. No fuss, no muss. Just plug in your affiliate URL address and the money starts rolling in.

Yeah, right…

If it was THAT easy, everyone would be financially successful online. The major problem with this particular sequence of events is the fact that you're not alone. Hundreds (if not thousands) of other individuals are also affiliates and are therefore promoting the very same products.

And not just the same products. They're most often promoting and marketing that product in the same exact way. You know… sign up as an affiliate, get an affiliate link, shove that affiliate link in front of as many eyes as possible.

Discussion board messages, signature files, newsletter ads, email campaigns… you name it, that affiliate URL is going to show up in every conceivable place online. Multiply that times the amount of people who are also promoting that same product and what you wind up with is a virtual flood.

And what usually happens with a flood? Rather than take an interest in the underlying facts surrounding the rush of water, victims spend most of their time and effort trying to avoid the onslaught.

Viewers see a URL address, click on it, read the sales copy, and then make a decision. They either purchase the product or move on. Whatever future flood of affiliate URL addresses they come across for that particular product will simply be avoided… after all, they've already been there, done that.

So what are the chances of your affiliate URL address being the first one most consumers happen to encounter? You guessed it… zero, zip, nada.

The truth is, there's only one way to successfully promote products as an affiliate (and coincidentally, the only way that works with EVERY conceivable product acquisition method). That is…

You need to present products from your own personal vantage point.

That equates to an online environment that only you have access to. One that you can use to place your own promotion efforts at a much higher level. One that allows you to stand out, allows you to be unique, allows you to step outside the standard already-flooding-the-market sales box.

Regardless of what information product you choose, regardless of how many other people might already be promoting any given product… it's absolutely imperative that you "sell" any and all products from web pages that you control.

Of course, if you're an affiliate for someone else, you'll technically be "pre-selling" their product. (The buyer will most often be directed to and then funneled through the product owner's sales letter and purchase process.) Even so, the set-up - getting the prospective buyer fired up and ready to purchase - should always be initiated from the page or pages of your own personal website.

What that affords you is the ability to be different, and to present a much more personal and targeted marketing effort. You can write your own sales copy, offer your own exclusive bonuses, include independent product testimonials… whatever you like.

The point is, the only truly successful money-making system (and one that will last long after you've initiated it) is one in which YOU maintain most of the control. And the only method where you can do that - and do that well - is from a website that's owned by you.

Now… the operative word here is "owned". Deliberately omitted were the words "and operated". That's because the Profit Equalizer system gives you the option of either taking care of everything yourself or working from a management position (outsourcing tasks to others).

What that equates to here is simple…

1. If you have the ability - and the time to do so - you can build your own product sites (and/or product sales pages on sites you already own and operate).

3. You can hire someone to do it for you. For that, the choices would include…

- Individual or company that creates websites.
- Individual or company that creates and maintains websites.
- Management firm that does everything from creating sites to marketing them.

If you want maximum results with the least amount of time and effort invested by you personally, hiring a management firm is definitely the way to go. In most instances, you hand them specific information (details about the product you're selling, the page design, and the content you want included) and they take it from there.

Once implemented, you also arrange for the type of ongoing traffic you want your site to receive as well as how much and how often. So the overall drill is this…

First, you do whatever research is necessary to determine which topic and product you'll be selling. You write (or hire someone to write for you) the sales copy and general content that will be included on your web pages.

Second, you turn all this specific information over to the management firm.

Third, the management firm creates the website (according to your specifications) and then implements whatever traffic and promotion methods have been agreed upon.

The basic services that most management marketing firms provide include creating, promoting, and maintaining sites. Some even offer additional services such as copywriting and purchase and delivery process. How much you hire them to do is entirely your choice.

Of course, if you don't feel you can afford to jump right in and commit to this type of paid arrangement, you need to handle all these tasks yourself - at least, until you get one or two systems up and running.

Once you have a couple of them under your belt (and they're generating a fair amount of steady income), you can take a more serious look at hiring someone else to manage all of these repetitive and oftentimes cumbersome operational details.

The important thing is that you need a good solid vantage point. And that vantage point is your own website from which to promote any chosen product. Whether you create and operate it yourself or hire someone else to do it for you doesn't really matter.

In order to generate substantial amounts of cash, you'll need the freedom and control necessary to present the product in a powerful and unique way.

Now… there's one other aspect to consider: Do you need to create a website for every product that you promote? Not necessarily.

If several of your products are somehow related, you could develop a general website that encompasses the overall category. For example, pet training manuals. Within that category, you would then create individual pages or specific areas of the website that pertain solely to each of the separate products… how to make your dog stop barking, how to teach your parrot to talk or perform tricks, how to get your cat to use the toilet bowl rather than a litter box.

What you need to understand is this… the power of the Profit Equalizer system is in the concept of selling individual digital products over and over again - with as little ongoing effort and maintenance as possible. Whether you decide to create separate websites that "showcase" each of those products or not, the system itself will still allow you to generate a substantial amount of income.

Next, we'll discuss the best methods for presenting information products.

Key No. 7: Present The Product

While it's true that information products are a hot commodity, it's also true that you have nothing to show your potential customers…

Unlike physical products where you can simply display photos, include a description, and list specific attributes (things like width, height, color, and texture), digital products are nothing more than files that are transferred from one computer to another. And that means you'll have to work harder to convey exactly what it is you're selling.

Yes, you'll most likely be including a 3D "cover" image, one that gives the impression the digital product is an actual book or report. And that's certainly a terrific visual aid, a means of showing the prospective buyer something tangible.

But that's not nearly enough. Your ultimate task is to properly convey to people what information they'll be receiving and how it will benefit them. And that's where good quality sales copy comes in.

Start with a compelling headline, one that captures the reader's attention and gets them thinking…

- "Does Your Parrot Just Sit There Eating Food And Making A Mess?"
- "Are Your Neighbors Fed Up Listening To Your Dog Bark All Night Long?"
- "Have You Ever Wished There Was A Litter Box That Could Clean Itself?"

And then add an even more compelling sub-headline:

- "In Just Two Short Weeks You Can Turn That Lazy Parrot Into An Energetic Performer That Will Constantly Amaze Your Family And Friends!"
- "One Simple Technique And Your Dog Will Sleep Peacefully Through The Night - And So Will You And Your Neighbors!"
- "Even Better… Now You Can Say 'Good-bye' To That Eyesore And NEVER Have To Clean Another Dirty Smelly

Litter Box Again!"

With regard to the sales copy itself, there are several trains of thought with regard to how it needs to be structured. For example, some feel that placing a great customer testimonial at the very top will establish the maximum degree of credibility. Others insist that more sales will be generated if the copy ends with one or two postscripts (PS…).

For the most part, you can generally let the headline determine the nature of the sales copy and how it will be presented. For example, if the headline posed a dilemma such as having a lazy, messy parrot on your hands, the sales copy could begin along that same vein. Basically, expanding on the problem which in turn leads to the solution… the information product that teaches your parrot to do unusual and entertaining tricks.

Another good sales copy starter is to convey a story or statistic that relates to the problem or dilemma.

Let's say, for example, that your headline is "Don't Be Another Lung Cancer Statistic - Safe Natural Herb Guarantees That You'll Stop Smoking Within 2 Weeks!".

You could then begin your sales copy with actual statistics… "Are you aware that 1 of out every 3 smokers will die of lung cancer before the age of 50? According to the latest issue of the *Cancer Research Medical Journal*…"

The point is, you don't want to lose any of the effect or momentum that the headline (and sub-headline) have created. Whatever direction the headline takes, use it as the basis for starting the actual sales copy.

Once you've accomplished that, introduce the reader to the information product itself. Then present the benefits they will gain from having access to that information (for example, experiencing a peaceful night's sleep, being the envy of all their parrot owner friends, never again having to clean another litter box).

In order to be effective, sales copy needs to lead the viewer through a pre-determined pattern of content which gradually escalates, ultimately reaching the point where the viewer feels compelled to click on the buy button.

The pre-determined pattern should start with a thought-provoking comment or question

> which leads to the primary problem that needs to be solved
> which leads to the solution of that problem
> which leads to a compelling reason to make the purchase.

Breaking it all down into specific areas, sales copy should include the following components in the following sequence:

1. A powerful opening (attention-grabbing headline and sub-headline).
2. An equally powerful introduction (such as a story or statistical information).
3. Sympathy and understanding (with regard to the problem, dilemma, or frustration the viewer is experiencing).
4. Product information (what it is, what kind of content it includes).
5. Benefits (a list of all the positive results the viewer will gain after having read and implemented the information).
6. The closing (a summation of the product and the benefit of purchasing it).
7. Call to action (giving the viewer a reason to purchase right away.

Which brings the viewer to the actual method of placing their purchase - the order link or button. Above all else, make it obvious, make it easy, and make it secure. And be certain that you clearly indicate how the purchase process will take place.

Also, since you're dealing in digital products, you should never automatically assume all viewers know how the delivery process takes place. Make it clear how and when the buyer will receive their product.

The best method, of course, would be to include a download link on the "thank you" page (where they are taken once the purchase process has been completed). This not only automates the delivery process, it gives the buyer yet another reason to order your product...

**Purchase Now And Get Immediate Access To
"Turn Your Lazy Parrot Into An Energetic Star"
Even If It's 2:00 AM In The Morning!**

Naturally, the sales copy you create will ultimately be placed on whatever web page you'll be using to promote the respective product. Whether you've hired a management firm or you plan to create the website and/or page yourself, it's important to showcase the product cleanly and professionally.

If the product will be promoted from it's own website, the best choice is the standard and most popular layout which includes a simple header graphic above a white content area (where the sales copy will be inserted).

If the product is being promoted on an existing website - where the page layout is a bit more involved - you'll naturally want to insert the sales copy in the main content area of the page. In other words, even though there might be things like other links, ads, or products displayed throughout the page, the primary content area should be devoted to the product that's currently being showcased and nothing else.

As previously mentioned, you can promote products individually or develop a general website from which multiple theme-related products are sold. The advantage of the second choice is that any viewer who comes to the site will most likely have an interest in the other products as well.

That means you have an opportunity to make more than one sale from a single buyer. For example, let's say you've chosen several products that teach people how to train their dog in one aspect or another (stop barking, stop biting, follow commands without a leash, stay within the confines of the yard, learn basic tricks, clicker training).

Initially, a dog owner might come to your web page because they're interested in one particular manual. Having seen all the additional training information you offer, there's a good chance they'll purchase another product - either right away or at some point in the future.

The other advantage is related to overall promotion. Although you'll need to generate traffic for specific words related to specific products, you'll also have the ability to generate generic dog interest traffic. Basically, the opportunity to target and ultimately attract anyone who happens to be involved with dogs.

Internet marketers refer to it as developing a "niche". And the truth is, if you can establish and develop a good one, you'll be guaranteed to generate substantial income for years to come.

And speaking of generating income, the next key will help you zero in on exactly the right direction to follow.

Key No. 8: Run A Consumer Test

Assuming you've got everything set up and ready to go for at least one of your information products (the web page, the sales copy, the order and delivery process), it's time to put all of your hard work to the test. And that is...

Let's see just how much money this product can generate.

In order to do that, you'll need to get traffic. But not just any traffic. What you need at this point (or any stage of promotion) is targeted viewers whose interest in this type of product is quite high. In other words, they're already standing on the brink of purchase.

Also, you need to summon those targeted viewers as soon as humanly possible. Time IS money, after all.

So what's the best and most effective method to accomplish both those goals? Simple... Google AdWords (http://adwords.google.com).

Beyond a doubt, this is THE most effective and targeted means of bringing pre-qualified buyers to your web page. Even more important, you can start receiving those viewers almost immediately. And that in itself is an extremely powerful marketing asset.

First and foremost, it affords you the ability to jump right in and see exactly what volume of interest a certain product will bring. Secondly, it allows you the possibility of generating income within hours (or even minutes) of implementing your ad campaign.

Assuming you don't know anything about it...

Google AdWords is the number one pay-per-click advertising program. And what does pay-per-click mean? You develop ads that are highly specific to the product you're selling and then, instead of paying upfront, you pay for actual visitors after they are received.

Here's how it works...

Through your account with Google AdWords, you arrange to place an ad in the *Sponsor Links* column of Google search result pages. That ad is linked to a certain keyword that you've specifically chosen. When a viewer clicks on that ad - and only when a viewer clicks on the ad - you are charged a per-click fee (which was pre-determined when you initially established that particular ad).

Since you only pay for the ad when someone actually clicks on it, the ad has the potential of either being a bargain method of advertising or being a virtual money pit. It's up to you to make certain it remains a bargain.

And here's how you do that…

There are several primary factors involved in operating a successful AdWords campaign and each of them is equally significant. That said, let's start by talking about the ad itself (since that will be responsible for attracting viewers in the first place).

Unlike other forms of advertising, whereby you do whatever is necessary in order to encourage people to see what you have to offer, pay-per-click ads require that you do just the opposite. And that is, you'll actually want to <u>discourage</u> people from clicking on your ad. Or, to put it more accurately, you want to discourage people who would NOT be interested in purchasing your product.

Remember, you'll be paying for each and every click that takes place. If you present the usual and openly generic ad, you run the risk of attracting all sorts of people who are merely curious and have no desire to purchase anything.

In order to prevent that from happening, it's important that you include the price of your information product - a definite no-no in any other form of advertising.

Normally, your goal would be to get countless viewers to the sales page by any and all possible means and then use your "killer" sales copy to convince them what a bargain they're getting. So the price is pretty much the LAST thing that would be presented to them.

When you're using pay-per-click ads, however, it's a whole different story. You want your ad to act as both a deterrent AND an attraction. Because each click is costing you money, you need to prevent non-buyers from clicking on the ad while at the same time giving serious buyers a qualified reason to take the next step.

Here's an example of including the price in a Google ad (where "parrot training" is the keyword)…

Fast & Easy Parrot Training
Turn Your Parrot Into A Star
Performer for only $24.95

With this type of ad, you immediately eliminate anyone and everyone who isn't prepared to pay "x" amount of dollars for your information product. So it definitely makes sense to show people the price right up front. Unless, of course…

You're absolutely, positively CERTAIN your sales copy will convert the average viewer into a buyer. Most likely, at this stage of the process, you couldn't possible count on that.

Keep in mind, this particular key is entitled "Run A Consumer Test". So what you should be aiming for is a very restrictive ad campaign, one that will truly indicate whether or not a certain product will generate a substantial amount of income.

You see, you already know the subject matter of the product will generate interest - that was the purpose of all the preliminary research. The only thing left to determine is the product's cash-flow potential.

Once you've determined that - once you've tested long enough to prove any given product is income worthy - you can then try different types of approaches with regard to the ads and ad content. (For example, the price up front versus not including the price at all.)

Another thing you should be aware of is the fact that Google doesn't give you much to work with in terms of ad space. In fact, the average ad only contains 12 to 15 words (including the title). So you need to be extremely creative - as well as cautious - when determining both the title and the text within your ad.

The best advice here is to conduct a search using some of your own primary keywords. Then look under *Sponsor Links* and see what wording is associated with the ads listed there. After a while, you'll begin to notice a pattern - how certain types of phrases are used in order to heighten viewer attention.

But again, you're not trying to solicit a vast amount of random viewers. You want a select number of highly targeted and pre-qualified potential buyers. So make certain your ad does, for the most part, eliminate those who are merely idle surfers.

Now… in order to receive maximum results from any ads that you run, it's always a good idea to conduct split tests. That's where you run two ads for the same product but one has something slightly different - like the title or a specific word.

For example, one ad might use the phrase "easy training method" while the other says "fast training method". The one that converts the most traffic into sales is naturally the winning ad. The point is, you need to test different ads as well as different targets. Which brings us to another significant factor… choosing keywords.

Overall, you can target as many keywords as you like. While conducting initial tests, however, you should limit yourself to no more than half a dozen keywords (the exact number will be determined by the product and the popularity and relevance of the keywords).

Although you might be tempted to target more than that, don't do it. At least, not yet. If you start right off the bat trying to create ads for more than a few keywords, your ads could suffer the consequences. You need to focus on a few keywords which will then allow you to concentrate on making the ads the best they can possibly be.

Of course, once you become comfortable creating these ad campaigns - and achieve a certain level of financial success - you can increase the volume of keywords as much as you like. Or, at the very least, as much as you feel you can properly handle - both physically and financially. The important thing is to not get ahead of yourself at the very beginning.

Remember... <u>one</u> step at a time.

Ok. Now back to the keywords themselves... just like when you conducted your initial research, you want keywords that:

- are being widely and heavily searched for
- don't already have too much competition
- can be acquired for a relatively low per-click price

Always keep in mind that general keywords most often cost more per click and generate the largest number of random viewers. On the other hand, more specific keywords will be less costly and will attract a smaller number of highly targeted viewers. Needless to say, the latter will average out to more cash profit in the long run.

There's no doubt about it... choosing the right keywords is going to require some work on your part, but it's definitely worth it. If you invest additional time and effort now, you'll be more likely to achieve maximum long-range income potential. (Take shortcuts and you'll continue to struggle along indefinitely.)

Here's the deal...

Google is the BEST method to test your entire sales process - getting targeted traffic, converting that traffic to income, expanding the advertising campaign. Beyond that, it's also the best method for improving and perfecting your entire sales process...

With most traffic generation strategies and systems, it can be a hit or miss prospect. And oftentimes it takes weeks or even months to experience any significant or valid results. With Google, however, you can be pulling in highly targeted and "willing to purchase" viewers within minutes of launching your campaign.

Plus... you can count on a steady stream of targeted viewers day after day, week after week, month after month. That means you can continue to test, examine, alter, adjust, tweak, and refine your ads, your headlines, your sales copy - until you reach the maximum level of cash flow.

And that equates to the most valuable key of all... one that gives you access to additional income steams any time you want. An unlimited cash machine which can be tapped into over and over again.

Assuming, of course, you continue to repeat the process. Which just happens to be the next key in the Profit Equalizer system.

Key No. 9: Repeat The Process

Here's a typical scenario…

A person comes online and locates a product, service, or program they feel is a promising money-maker. After promoting the heck out of it, they do manage to experience a certain degree of financial success. Unfortunately, since the amount doesn't equate to the dollar figure they feel they need in order to quit their job and work online fulltime, they drop the product and move on to something else.

Or, they just give up entirely, assuming that making a living solely via the internet can't possibly be done.

That's what generally happens when you place all the financial burden on one product or solitary online business venture. So what should you do instead? Always, ALWAYS, develop multiple avenues from which to generate income.

And with the Profit Equalizer system, that means selling numerous digital information products. That way, if one product begins to generate less income (or fails completely), you still have others that will collectively bring in a substantial and steady cash flow.

So let's say you get a product set up and the average profit that's generated is only $100 a week. Should you forget about that product or keep promoting it? You should definitely keep promoting it. Why? Because some products will generate large amounts of income while others will generate more modest amounts.

What matters is your collective income - the sum of all the products put together. And unless the income from a particular product drops so dramatically that you're experiencing very little profit, there's no reason not to continue promoting it.

Rather than look at a single product as the answer to your financial goal, you need to see it as merely a piece of the entire treasure. And, as long as there are numerous products involved, those individual pieces will always add up to a considerable amount of income.

Don't forget... once you get a product up and running, it merely requires a small amount of attention and/or maintenance. That in turn gives you the opportunity to set up yet another product system.

And that's exactly what the most financially successful online marketers do... the moment they've established a solid cash flow, they turn right around and begin researching and developing even more cash flows.

And why not? Once the first system is in place, you've pretty much got the whole process honed down to a finely-tuned machine. After that, it's simply a matter of repeating everything you've previously done - not once, not twice, but as many times as you want. And of course, the more times you repeat the process, the more cash flow you'll experience.

Just be aware that the first time you go through the process will be the toughest, especially if you're not familiar or experienced with certain aspects. In that case, it will take you a bit longer to get everything up and running. But again, once you accomplish that, it's clear sailing from that point on...

None of the additional product sales systems will require anything new or unusual. It's comprised of tasks that you've already accomplished, events that you've already set in motion. So naturally, repeating those tasks will come easier each time you perform them.

The important thing is knowing that each product will generate a certain amount of cash flow. And each cash flow will contribute to the total sum of income you take in.

So... if your daily financial goal is $100 a day and you've got two product systems in place which bring in a total of $50 a day, you know that it will most likely take two more products before you can reach your first financial goal.

Of course, you could very well get a single product system going that brings in enough money to meet or even exceed your initial financial goal. It does happen. And the more research you put into choosing your first product, the more likely you are to see that kind of income right from the start.

The only thing you don't want to do is become discouraged if your first product falls somewhat short of your expectations. Get the cash flowing and then move on to the next product.

The truth is, many of your most profitable product ideas will reveal themselves while you're conducting research for some other product. So it's not just the final cash flows that determine the success of the system… it's the process of actively studying the market, seeking out new niches or areas of interest, and then putting an associated product out there for targeted viewers to find (and ultimately purchase).

If you do that - and repeat the process over and over again - there's no limit to the amount of income you can generate. Not just initially, but for years to come.

So what's left after you repeat the process of choosing products and bringing in additional cash flows? That would be the methods by which you can expand on the system. And that's exactly what we'll delve into next.

Key No. 10: Expand The Scope Of Your Operation

If you never do anything more than implement the first nine keys of the Profit Equalizer system, you'll always be guaranteed a steady online income. Of course, most people don't stop there. Especially when they see their bank account balance steadily and constantly rising.

You see, when you don't have much money, you're likely to envision the kind of money that would afford you the ability to upgrade the things you have - a larger home, nicer furniture, a better car, designer clothes.

Once that level of financial success is within reach, however, most people begin to imagine an even greater potential - an exotic and exciting lifestyle, trips around the globe, private jets and limousines, hobnobbing with the rich and famous.

So what began as a dream has evolved into something that's actually attainable. And when that kind of notion sinks in, the reaction most people have is simple and direct... the burning desire to generate even MORE income.

It's kind of like that Pringles' commercial slogan... *once you pop you can't stop*.

Once you see all that money rolling in, you can't stop yourself from wanting to generate additional income. Quite simply, it's addictive. And like any addition, you can never seem to get enough of what makes you feel good... in this case, money!

So let's see what we can do in order to drive these already high profit generators up to the next level.

Additional Products

There's no question that you should keep digital information products as the central core of your profit-generating systems. After all, there will always be a vast and diversified number of them available to fuel your systems. Not to mention the fact that they've proven time and time again to bring in extraordinary amounts of income.

But that doesn't mean you should exclude the possibility of venturing beyond information products. Software programs, for example, have many of the same desirable characteristics - they can be delivered digitally, they cover a wide variety of interest areas, and they're extremely popular throughout online buyers.

Plus, they can easily generate ten times the amount of money you make from information products. Why? Simply because they carry higher price tags.

But before you drop everything in search of great software products, it's important for you to realize that selling software products generally takes much more time (tech support alone can be very time-consuming) and effort than information products.

The cost for most of the information products that you'll be selling will fall within the twenty-five to fifty dollar range. With the right specialized software products, you could be looking at a price of anywhere from a hundred dollars all the way up to a thousand.

Conceivably, you could sell one software product and make more money than having sold ten information products. Needless to say, that's quite a difference in monetary gain. However…

When you're dealing in high-dollar items, you need to realize that people have a greater tendency NOT to buy anything the first time around. In other words, you can't just send them to your sales page and expect them to purchase right away.

Instead, you'll need to have a long-range sales opportunity, one that will afford you the ability to contact them directly over an extended period of time (weeks or even months beyond the day they initially came to your website).

The best way to do that efficiently is to set up an autoresponder system whereby they automatically receive promotional emails from you at preset intervals. That way, you can continue to promote your software product without having to manually contribute any more of your time.

What type of messages do you send? What works best for software are tips and information on the benefits of using that particular program. For example, if you're selling a product like Ad Word Analyzer, you could periodically send them a series of real-life instances where the program helped someone locate a particular niche that in turn brought them substantial income.

Or, you could simply send them valuable tips on how the program can improve their ability to develop new and highly profitable income streams.

Or, you could do both, sending them two messages each week... one includes a real-life example of success, the other presenting a tip on how to benefit from the program.

Now... whether you decide to move up to software products or not, implementing autoresponder messages is a great and highly profitable expansion method. Make sure you seriously consider it for all your information products.

Naturally, before you can even send out autoresponder messages, you'll need the person's name and email address. Which brings us to one of the most important areas of expanding ANY online business venture.

Establish Your Own Mailing List

The most important and valuable names you can have on any list are those of your paying customers. Basically, people who have already purchased something from you.

Without a doubt, they are the easiest prospects when it comes to promoting yet another product - especially if it's related to their initial topic of interest. For example, the dog training manuals. They purchased one of your information products, therefore, there's a very high possibility they'll purchase another.

How soon they purchase another product might be entirely up to you.

You see, if left entirely alone, they could simply disappear into cyberspace. (It's not uncommon for people to forget where they purchased something online, especially when that something is digital.)

But let's say you have individual product autoresponders set up. Each time someone purchases a training manual, they automatically receive a series of messages about that product. You know, tips and information, examples of how best to use the information. That kind of thing.

Now... within each of those messages, you also cleverly promote your other dog training manuals - stop barking, stop chewing, obey off-leash commands. That way, they keep being gently bombarded with your website address as well as the opportunity to add yet another quality information product to their arsenal of training tools.

So you can see how important it is to keep in touch with people who have already purchased from you. Of course, the fact that they've purchased from you online means you automatically acquired their name and email address.

But what about all those prospective buyers who come to your website and then wind up leaving empty-handed?

For that, you need to actively solicit their personal information. And the best method of accomplishing that is to offer them something for free (that's directly related to the product you're selling) in exchange for their name and email address.

The free something can be a report, an e-course (a series of autoresponder messages), or even a small script or software program. Whatever you can come up with will do the job. Just make certain it's valuable enough to actually warrant someone giving you their name and email address.

The last thing you want is to have someone angry or upset that the freebie you used to get their personal information is useless or of no value whatsoever.

Remember, the purpose of having someone on your list is to encourage them to either purchase a first product from you or to get an established customer to spend even more money on additional products that you're offering (or will be offering in the future).

The best method of acquiring names and email addresses is through a simple form on your website. And it should be placed on all appropriate web pages, not just the home page.

Just make certain that you explain how their personal information will be used. And make it perfectly clear right up front that you'll be sending them follow-up messages. If you don't, they could easily accuse you of spamming them.

But don't worry. Being totally honest won't discourage qualified individuals from giving you their name and email address. Not if you let them know that the information you'll be sending them is valuable to their particular interest.

And what about anyone who <u>would</u> be discouraged? That's fine too. They're just your typical random surfer looking for a chance to get something for free. And you certainly don't need that type of person on your list.

<u>Develop Your Own Products</u>

The highest level of income possibilities you can reach are those in which you pocket the entire share of the money that's being generated.

As an affiliate or a joint venture partner, you'll always be splitting income with someone else. And although you can certainly amass a tremendous amount of wealth that way, you might be more comfortable operating totally independent of anyone else.

Of course, that means you would also need to develop your own products. That might seem like it involves a great deal of work, but the truth is, it's really doesn't. If anything, it frees you to pursue much more diversified areas of interest.

How so? Well, let's say you're conducting keyword research on a particular area of the health industry. You find a niche that is not only capable of producing a tremendous amount of income, it's virtually untapped. The only problem is, you can't locate a suitable product that will fill the demand.

Normally, you would simply scratch that one off your list of possibilities. Or, at the very least, put it off to the side in case you somehow stumble across a suitable product somewhere down the line.

But what about creating your own custom product? One that fills the demand exactly and completely? Wouldn't that be the ultimate solution? You bet it would. And the good news is, it can be accomplished with little effort on your part. And, for a lot less money than you would assume.

In case you're not aware, there are services available where business owners and professional workers come together with the purpose of hiring and be hired. Basically, they're the online version of real-world employment agencies like Manpower and Allied Forces…

Businesses post jobs and services that they need filled. Professionals post their portfolios and bid on open projects.

Go to websites like Elance (http://www.elance.com) and Script Lance (http://www.scriptlance.com) and you'll see a wide variety of open projects as well as the bids and feedback that relates to the professionals who are hoping to be hired for those jobs.

Whether you need a specific software program or information book created, or a report, or e-course written, you're sure to find the right person to do that. And the best part is, you'll have numerous people competing for your project. That means you can almost always get a good deal on whatever job you list there.

So aside from submitting a project and deciding which professional should get the job, what do you yourself need to contribute? Just the initial keyword and product research and preliminary investigation. The same type of work you would be conducting for any other income-producing system you're looking into.

Well, there you have it. Methods to expand on the Profit Equalizer system, allowing you to drive it to an even higher financial level. Which brings us to the only thing that's left for you to do... get your Profit Equalizer system moving!

The sooner you do, the sooner you'll get to enjoy that wonderful and free-living lifestyle you've always dreamed about.

May the fortune <u>always</u> be with you!